TO:

FROM:

Copyright © 2019 by Annette Bridges

www.annettebridges.com

Published by Ranch House Press

All rights reserved. Except as permitted under the U.S. Copyright Act of 1976, no part of this publication may be reproduced, distributed, or transmitted in any form or by any means, or stored in a database or retrieval system, without the prior written permision of the author.

Illustrated by Lesley Vernon
www.lvdesignhouse.com

Layout and Cover Design by Janie Owen-Bugh
www.janieowenbugh.com

Printed in the United States of America.

ISBN 978-1-946371-43-0

A DACHSHUND TALE

BY ANNETTE BRIDGES

LESSONS LEARNED FROM MY DOG

INTRODUCTION

The loss of our furry loved ones may be the hardest of all, especially when we're faced with the decision to help them cross their rainbow bridge. I've been having trouble catching my breath ever since my last moments with my precious little Lady. What I have found helpful is pondering all the ways my life has been graced by her presence. The creation of this little book is the outcome.

I was blessed with seventeen years of being loved by her. Lady's was a lifetime of a spirit often stronger than her body and due to this, she gifted me with many life lessons for which I will be eternally grateful.

Perhaps among the greatest lessons was how she dealt with her struggles. She had her first seizure when only one year old. I will forever be in awe of how she could have a horrific episode and an hour later act like nothing had happened. She had the ability to totally move on with the business of living and playing and enjoying herself in spite of her challenges and limitations. I so want to be like her!

She had a disc rupture in her back when she was ten years old that left her backside totally paralyzed. Surgery and months of therapy resulted in her walking again. I can't help but smile when I think of the many weeks we had to raise her backside and legs up with a towel while she walked with her front legs. She often paused and looked back at me as if to say, "Ummm Mom, can you please walk a little faster and keep up?" She was like a miniature canine Marine who learned to improvise, adapt and overcome whatever confronted her.

We often referred to her as a little trooper. She was that and so much more! Nothing daunted her. Nothing stopped her. Over time, she may have moved a little slower and a bit less gracefully, but she kept going, doing the best she could. The main point is, she kept going.

She loved to eat what she liked. She loved to play when she was in the mood. She took long naps and enjoyed a good stretch and wiggle when she woke up. She was fiercely independent but always enjoyed snuggles with her mommy and daddy. She made me feel totally and unconditionally loved and I adored her with my whole heart.

This book is dedicated to my sweet Lady. I wanted to pay tribute to the blessings she gave to me and share them with others in the hopes you will be inspired by her, too. Mostly, I wanted to invite others who may be grieving the loss of their furry beloved to spend some time pondering the ways your life has been touched by your sweet one. I've found it to be a way to turn sadness into celebration. I hope you find it helpful as well.

A friend recently spoke of her furry baby who had passed as her heart's companion. I love that term of endearment. It's so fitting, so true. It's never easy to say goodbye to our heart's companion. How could it be? If we have loved well, then undoubtedly we will need to grieve well. But I do think a powerful tool to do just that is to consider every way we are grateful for the furry friends in our lives.

How comforted we can be by valuing and treasuring what their life meant to ours and how we were changed and inspired by their presence. I believe this keeps our furry loved ones unforgettable in our hearts as the jewels they will forever be.

Meet Little Lady Bridges. Little Lady was never in a hurry when she went outside to go potty. She didn't let anyone or anything rush her while she searched for the perfect spot.

DON'T BE IN TOO BIG A HURRY.

TAKE TIME TO SMELL EVERY BLADE OF GRASS.

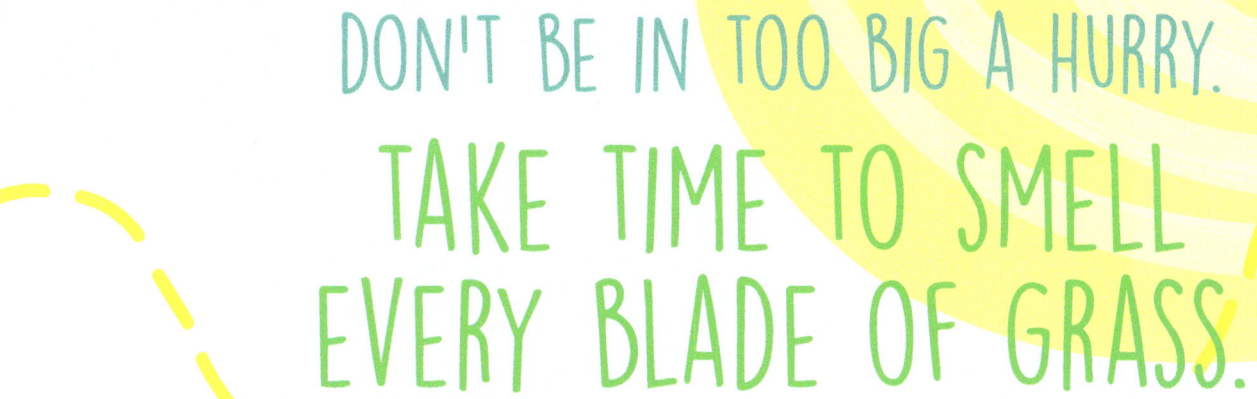

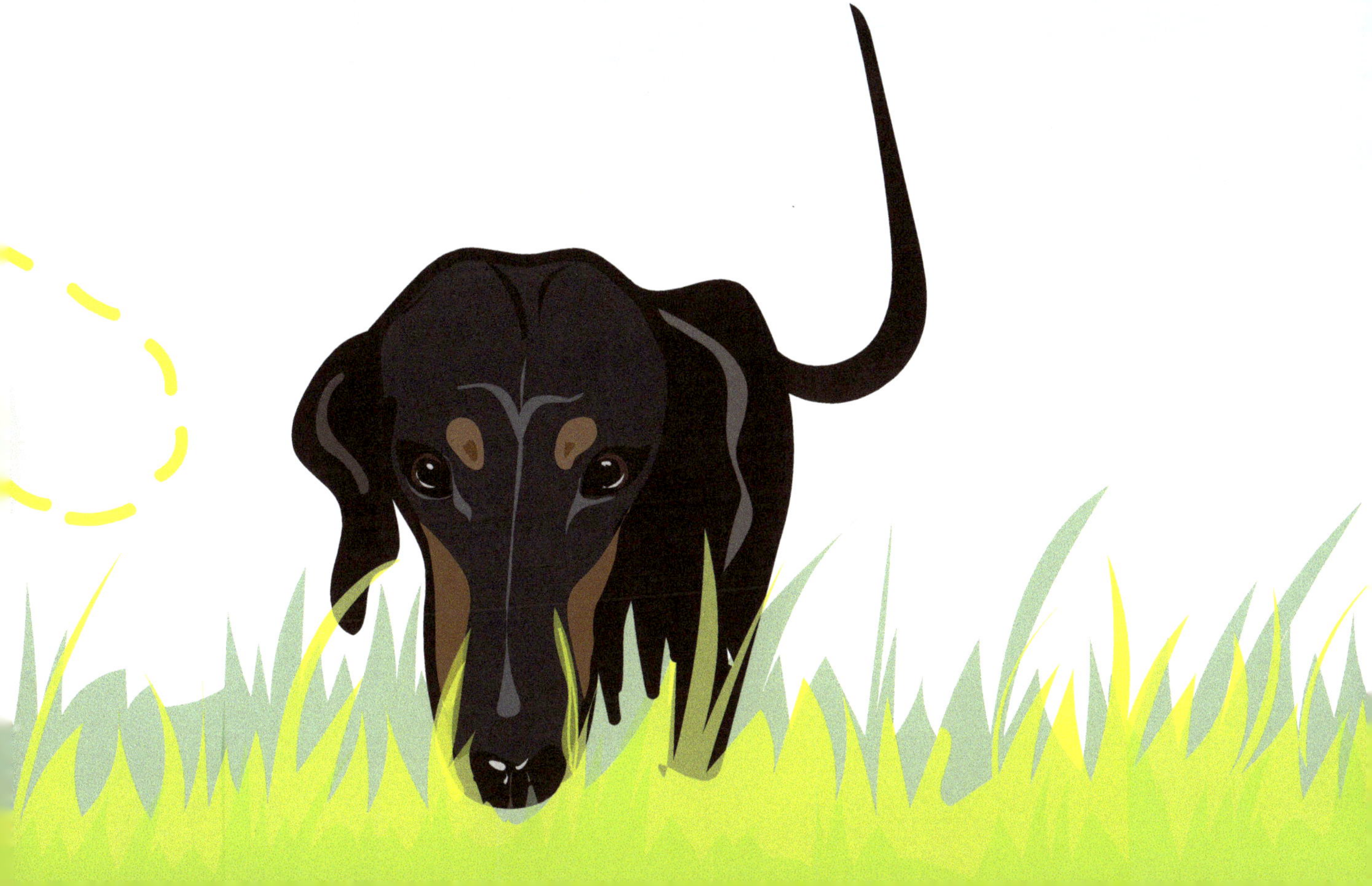

Being a sickly doxie, there were many unpleasant events and experiences in Lady's long life. But no matter what, as soon as she felt better, she went immediately back to playing, eating and sleeping as if nothing bad ever happened.

There was absolutely no way that Lady was going outside in the rain and get her furry coat wet. But sometimes a gal can't wait for the rain to stop. And with a little help from her friends she found out that she didn't have to.

IT'S OKAY TO ASK FOR HELP.

THAT'S HOW YOU STAY DRY WHEN YOU HAVE TO GO OUT IN THE RAIN.

Lady loved trips to the ocean and was perfectly happy to sit in her beach chair for hours wrapped in her towel and taking deep breaths while basking in the warm and toasty sunshine.

Lady was grateful for her mom and dad's help while she recovered from back surgery, even though she did often wish they could walk a bit faster to keep up with her front legs.

Lady knew, like all dachshunds, that the best way to be ready to tackle whatever was required of you was to be well rested.

Lady was an awesome little traveler. She was excited to explore the scents and sights everywhere she went. Of course, she was always happy to be with those she loved most.

Little Lady was never too old to enjoy a delightful squeaky toy.

Whether she was digging through a pile of clothes, an open suitcase on the floor or in sand at the beach, Lady was relentlessly certain there was something to be found.

SOMETIMES YOU MUST DIG FOR BURIED TREASURE.

No matter what I said to little Lady, even in my darkest moments when I cried by her side, her sweet way of giving me her undivided attention made me feel totally understood and loved.

Lady didn't require lots of fancy toys to have fun. She found joy in the simplest of things. She knew happiness could be found right where we are.

In her youthful years, Lady loved to move as fast as she could. But even as a senior, she never stopped enjoying a brief sprint to chase a barn cat or rabbit.

Little Lady wanted everyone to know when she was happy. She knew the secret to making others happy was spreading her joy freely and generously.

When Lady met you at the door when you came home, you had no doubt you were the most cherished person in her world. It's pretty amazing to feel wanted and missed by a furry friend.

Being loved by my precious little Lady has truly been an unsurpassed, breathtaking and wonderful feeling of being completely, unconditionally and eternally loved. She will remain forever in my heart!

TO LOVE AND BE LOVED.
THAT REALLY IS
ALL YOU
NEED.

ACKNOWLEDGEMENTS

There are many I would like to acknowledge in the creating of this book.

I'm going to begin with being grateful that I followed my heart's urging. The writing of this book became a necessary tool to help me take much needed deep breaths and find a reason to smile when smiling ever again felt impossible. I think our heart really does always know what's best.

I thank my gifted and accomplished illustrator Lesley Vernon who first said yes to help me create this book at record-breaking speed. She was able to take my memories and bring them to life again. Lesley, your illustrations are a precious gift to me. It was like Christmas morning every time an illustration landed in my email box for review. You gave me smiles through my tears. You brought Lady back to life on every page and made her life eternal in this book.

I thank my brilliant and skillful graphic designer Janie Owen-Bugh who was masterly in her layout and adorable cover design for my book. You have brightened my dark time with the book's whimsical feeling. You, too, have accomplished greatness at record-breaking speed and brought my precious Lady back to me to hold forever in my hands.

I thank both my editor Laura Matthews and my daughter Jennifer Bridges who freely shared their suggestions and advice that helped me frame my words into sweet memories and treasured lessons learned.

I thank my dear husband John who went above and beyond always in his love and care for our sweet little Lady. Honey, she loved you dearly. I hope this book brings you some measure of comfort. Our Lady will live forever in our hearts. I'm grateful to have shared these memories with you. Thank you for bringing the gift of Lady's love into my life.

I thank every friend, and you all know who you are, that have listened to me through my tears and made me feel heard, understood, loved and cared for. You have given me the encouragement I needed during my darkest of days. To lose both my mom and dog within a month of each other has almost been unbearable but your friendships have given me the strength I most desperately needed.

And I simply must thank those who have been brave and thoughtful enough to share their own journey through grief and loss on social media. Your testimonies gave me hope through every agonizing step I've taken through my own sadness. You and your stories are appreciated more than you may ever know.